Note

Numbers in the text and tables may not add up to totals because of rounding.

Contents

Macroeconomic Effects of Alternative Budgetary Paths

Summary
Federal debt held by the public now exceeds 70 percent of the nation's annual output (gross domestic product, or GDP) and stands at a higher percentage than in any year since 1950. Under an assumption whereby current laws generally remain unchanged, federal debt will be 77 percent of GDP in 2023, the Congressional Budget Office (CBO) projects.[1] Such a large amount of federal debt will reduce the nation's output and income below what would occur if the debt was smaller, and it raises the risk of a fiscal crisis (in which the government would lose the ability to borrow money at affordable interest rates). Moreover, the aging of the population and rising health care costs will tend to push debt even higher in the following decades.

In addition, those projections of debt under current law incorporate scheduled changes in policies that will serve to restrain the growth of debt. For example, under current law, some significant tax provisions will expire at the end of this year or in later years, increasing revenues; automatic spending cuts included in the Budget Control Act of 2011 and modified in the American Taxpayer Relief Act of 2012 will go into effect on March 1, 2013; and Medicare's payment rates for physicians' services will fall in January 2014. If future legislation prevented those changes from taking effect and did not make other policy changes with offsetting budgetary effects, federal debt would be considerably higher than the amount projected under current law.

To aid lawmakers in assessing the macroeconomic effects of possible changes in tax and spending policies, this report describes the effects of three alternative budgetary paths: one with deficits that are greater than those projected under current law and two with deficits that are smaller. Those paths are purely illustrative and do not represent recommendations by CBO.

In evaluating policy changes that would change projected budget deficits, lawmakers would undoubtedly weigh other considerations besides the macroeconomic effects—taking into account, for example, views about the proper size of the federal government and the best allocation of its resources. Lawmakers would also be concerned about the distributional implications of proposed changes—that is, who would bear the burden of any cuts in spending or increases in taxes (or who would benefit from spending increases or tax cuts), and who would gain or lose from changes in economic conditions. Such considerations are outside the scope of this analysis but have been addressed by CBO in other reports.[2]

What Budgetary Paths Did CBO Analyze?
CBO analyzed three budgetary paths that would alter cumulative primary deficits (that is, deficits excluding interest costs) from 2014 to 2023 relative to those under current law—an increase of $2 trillion (Path 1), a decrease of $2 trillion (Path 2), and a decrease of $4 trillion (Path 3). In each case, the budgetary changes would begin in 2014 and increase steadily over time.

The changes in primary deficits that occurred under the three paths would induce changes in debt service (the interest the government pays on its debt). They would also affect the economy, which would have further budgetary consequences (mostly through the rate of economic growth and interest rates). As a result, CBO estimates, the changes in total deficits and in federal debt

---

1. See Congressional Budget Office, *The Budget and Economic Outlook: Fiscal Years 2013 to 2023* (February 2013).

2. See, for instance, Congressional Budget Office, *Choices for Deficit Reduction* (November 2012).

Figure 1.

Debt Held by the Public Under Current Law and the Illustrative Paths, Including Economic Effects, Fiscal Years 2013 to 2023

(Percentage of GDP)

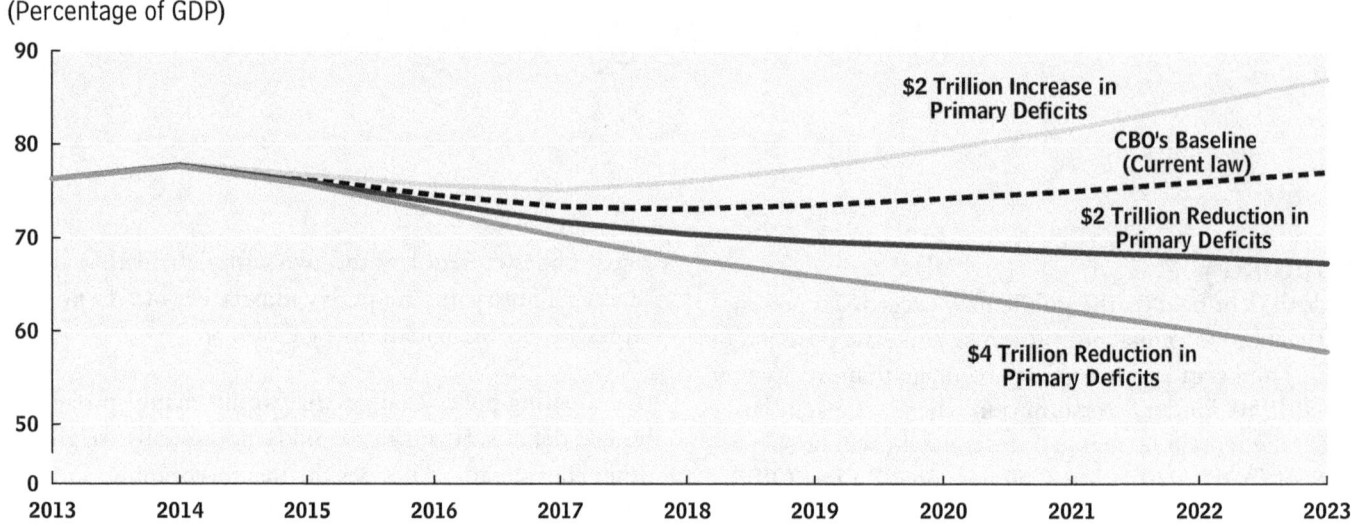

Source: Congressional Budget Office.

Notes: The illustrative paths are described in detail in the text, at the beginning of the section titled "Budget Deficits Under Three Illustrative Paths."

         The primary deficit equals revenues minus noninterest spending.

         GDP = gross domestic product.

held by the public from 2014 through 2023 would be as follows:

■ *Path 1: A $2 Trillion Increase in Primary Deficits.* With economic effects and debt service included, the cumulative increase in the deficit would total $2.5 trillion and debt would reach 87 percent of GDP in 2023, compared with, respectively, 73 percent at the end of 2012 and 77 percent projected for fiscal year 2023 under current law (see Figure 1).

■ *Path 2: A $2 Trillion Reduction in Primary Deficits.* The total cumulative decrease in the deficit would amount to $2.4 trillion and debt would drop to 67 percent of GDP in fiscal year 2023.[3]

---

3. The effects on output and interest rates of an increase in the deficit are larger than those of an equal-sized decrease in the deficit. As a result, the overall budgetary impact (including economic effects) of Path 1 is greater than that of Path 2 despite the fact that they begin with the same cumulative change in primary deficits. See Appendix A for details.

■ *Path 3: A $4 Trillion Reduction in Primary Deficits.* The total cumulative decrease in the deficit would amount to $4.8 trillion and debt would drop to 58 percent of GDP in fiscal year 2023.

For the sake of simplicity and to avoid any presumption about what particular policies might be chosen to reduce the deficit, CBO has not specified fiscal policies underlying the three illustrative paths. As a result, the projected outcomes under the three paths reflect no direct changes to the incentives to work and save that exist under current law; for example, marginal tax rates (the rates that apply to an additional dollar of a taxpayer's income) are assumed to be the same as those under current law. Therefore, the estimated macroeconomic effects presented in this report arise solely from the differences in deficits, and not from any effects of different tax policies or benefit programs that would directly alter people's incentives to work and save.

In fact, changing budget deficits significantly relative to what would occur under current law without altering incentives to work and save would be very difficult. If policies that raised or lowered deficits affected those incentives, then the overall economic impact of those policies would depend on both the changes in federal borrowing and the changes in incentives. In addition, the short-run economic impact of deficits would differ depending on how the specific tax and spending policies affected aggregate demand.[4]

How Would Such Budgetary Paths Affect the Economy?

In assessing the effects of the budgetary paths on total economic output, CBO focused on changes in gross national product (GNP). Unlike the more commonly cited GDP, GNP excludes foreigners' earnings on investments in the domestic economy but includes U.S. residents' earnings overseas; changes in GNP are therefore a better measure of the effects of policies on U.S. residents' income than are changes in GDP.

Relative to projections under current law, CBO estimates, policies that led to larger deficits by raising spending or cutting taxes would boost GNP from 2014 to 2016, and policies that reduced deficits by cutting spending or raising taxes would lower GNP in those years—reflecting the short-term impact of tax and spending policies on the demand for goods and services. By contrast, sustained higher deficits would lead to lower GNP beginning in 2017, and sustained lower deficits would lead to higher GNP beginning then—reflecting the impact of deficits on national saving and domestic investment (and without accounting for any changes to households' incentives to work or save stemming from changes to tax policies or benefit programs).

Compared with the agency's baseline projections (reflecting current law), the illustrative paths would have differing effects on GNP at the end of next year and after a decade:

■ *Path 1: A $2 Trillion Increase in Primary Deficits.* Real (inflation-adjusted) GNP would be higher, by 0.3 per-

cent, in the fourth quarter of 2014 and lower, by 0.9 percent, in 2023 than it would be under current law (see Table 1).

■ *Path 2: A $2 Trillion Reduction in Primary Deficits.* Real GNP would be lower, by 0.3 percent, in the fourth quarter of 2014 and higher, by 0.9 percent, in 2023 than it would be under current law.

■ *Path 3: A $4 trillion Reduction in Primary Deficits.* Real GNP would be lower, by 0.6 percent, in the fourth quarter of 2014 and higher, by 1.7 percent, in 2023 than it would be under current law.

Those findings represent CBO's central estimates, but to reflect the high degree of uncertainty involved, the agency also estimated a range of effects encompassing a broad span of economists' views about the relevant economic relationships.

Of course, policy changes of many other sizes and different patterns over time are possible, as are combinations of policies. For example, if policymakers wanted to raise GNP in the near term relative to projections under current law, as well as raise GNP in later years relative to that same benchmark, they could enact a combination of policies that increased deficits during the next few years and decreased them by a greater cumulative amount thereafter (ultimately leading to less debt than would arise under current law). That approach, however, would allow more federal debt to accumulate over the next few years and might raise doubts about whether long-term deficit reduction would actually take place. Households, businesses, state and local governments, and participants in the financial markets would be more likely to believe that the deficit reduction would truly take effect in the future if the future policy changes were specific and widely supported.

Budget Deficits Under Three Illustrative Paths

The three paths analyzed by CBO vary in the magnitude and direction of their budgetary changes but are phased in with the same timing. The impact of the paths is shown in terms of both the *primary budget deficit*, which is the difference between revenues and noninterest spending (excluding the costs of servicing the government's debt), and the *total deficit*, which is the difference between revenues and all spending. In

---

4. For examples of CBO's analysis of all of those effects of specific policies, see Congressional Budget Office, *Economic Effects of Policies Contributing to Fiscal Tightening in 2013* (November 2012), *The Long-Term Budget Outlook* (June 2012), *The Economic Impact of the President's 2013 Budget* (April 2012), *Policies for Increasing Growth and Employment in 2012 and 2013* (November 2011), and *The Economic Outlook and Fiscal Policy Choices* (September 2010).

Table 1.

Effects of Illustrative Paths on Real GNP in Selected Calendar Years, Relative to Projections Under Current Law

(Percentage difference)

	Short Term (2014)	Longer Term (2023)
$2 Trillion Increase in Primary Deficits		
Central estimate	0.3	-0.9
Range	0.1 to 0.5	-1.3 to -0.5
$2 Trillion Reduction in Primary Deficits		
Central estimate	-0.3	0.9
Range	-0.5 to -0.1	0.5 to 1.3
$4 Trillion Reduction in Primary Deficits		
Central estimate	-0.6	1.7
Range	-1.0 to -0.2	0.9 to 2.5

Source: Congressional Budget Office.

Notes: The illustrative paths are described in detail in the text, at the beginning of the section titled "Budget Deficits Under Three Illustrative Paths."

The primary deficit equals revenues minus noninterest spending.

Figures reflect the percentage difference (in the fourth quarter levels) between a path's effects and the outcomes under CBO's baseline, which incorporates the assumption that current laws generally remain unchanged.

Ranges of estimated effects are shown to reflect the uncertainty that exists about many of the economic relationships that are important in the models used to calculate those effects.

Real GNP = inflation-adjusted gross national product.

addition, total deficits are shown both excluding and including the macroeconomic impact of the changes in budget deficits. The effect of a policy change on the primary deficit excluding the macroeconomic effects is the number that would be provided in a standard CBO cost estimate for a legislative proposal. The effect of a policy change on the total deficit including the overall economic impact corresponds to the change in the deficit that would be included in CBO's baseline projections once that policy change was incorporated into the baseline. (Of course, an updated baseline would also include the effects of other legislative actions, other changes in the economic projections, and changes in the agency's technical assumptions.)

Path 1: A $2 Trillion Increase in Primary Deficits
Cumulatively over fiscal years 2014 to 2023, deficits under Path 1 would exceed those under current law by $2.3 trillion—consisting of a $2.0 trillion increase in primary deficits and a $0.3 trillion increase in interest costs (see Table 2). The increases in primary deficits would

begin at $40 billion in fiscal year 2014 and rise steadily, reaching $360 billion in fiscal year 2023. (Those budgetary changes, as well as those in the descriptions of Paths 2 and 3 below, do not include the budgetary impact of the economic effects of the paths, which are discussed in later sections of the report.)

Path 2: A $2 Trillion Reduction in Primary Deficits
Path 2 is a mirror image of Path 1: Cumulatively, over fiscal years 2014 to 2023, deficits under Path 2 would fall below those under current law by $2.3 trillion—consisting of a $2.0 trillion decrease in primary deficits and a $0.3 billion decrease in interest costs. The decreases in primary deficits would begin at $40 billion in fiscal year 2014 and rise steadily, reaching $360 billion in fiscal year 2023.

Path 3: A $4 Trillion Reduction in Primary Deficits
Path 3 doubles the budgetary changes of Path 2. Cumulatively, over fiscal years 2014 to 2023, deficits under

Table 2.

Effects of Illustrative Paths on the Budget Without Economic Effects, Relative to Projections Under Current Law, Fiscal Years 2014 to 2023

(Billions of dollars)

	2014	2015	2016	2017	2018	2019	2020	2021	2022	2023	2014-2023
					Increases (-) in Deficits						
$2 Trillion Increase in Primary Deficits											
Effect on primary deficits	-40	-76	-111	-147	-182	-218	-253	-289	-324	-360	-2,000
Debt service	0	-1	-4	-10	-20	-29	-41	-55	-72	-91	-322
Effect on total deficits	-40	-76	-115	-156	-202	-247	-294	-344	-396	-451	-2,322
					Decreases (+) in Deficits						
$2 Trillion Reduction in Primary Deficits											
Effect on primary deficits	40	76	111	147	182	218	253	289	324	360	2,000
Debt service	0	1	4	10	20	29	41	55	72	91	322
Effect on total deficits	40	76	115	156	202	247	294	344	396	451	2,322
$4 Trillion Reduction in Primary Deficits											
Effect on primary deficits	80	151	222	293	364	436	507	578	649	720	4,000
Debt service	1	1	8	19	39	58	81	111	144	182	643
Effect on total deficits	81	152	230	312	404	493	588	688	793	902	4,643
Memorandum:											
CBO's February 2013 Baseline											
Primary deficit (-) or surplus	-373	-158	-153	-123	-88	-117	-131	-123	-163	-120	-1,549
Net interest (-)	-243	-272	-323	-412	-517	-593	-667	-730	-795	-857	-5,410
Total deficit	-616	-430	-476	-535	-605	-710	-798	-854	-957	-978	-6,958

Source: Congressional Budget Office.

Notes: The illustrative paths are described in detail in the text, at the beginning of the section titled "Budget Deficits Under Three Illustrative Paths."

       The primary deficit equals revenues minus noninterest spending. Debt service is the change in the deficit that would result from changes in the amount of interest paid on the public debt. The effect on total deficits is the sum of the effect on primary deficits and debt service.

       Negative numbers indicate that deficits under the path are larger than those under CBO's baseline, which incorporates the assumption that current laws generally remain unchanged; positive amounts indicate that deficits are smaller.

Path 3 would fall below those under current law by $4.6 trillion—consisting of a $4.0 trillion decrease in primary deficits and a $0.6 billion decrease in interest costs. The decreases in primary deficits would begin at $80 billion in fiscal year 2014 and rise steadily, reaching $720 billion in fiscal year 2023.

CBO's Analytical Approach
CBO used two approaches to estimate the economic effects of the three illustrative paths relative to the agency's February 2013 baseline economic forecast,

which incorporates the assumption that current laws generally remain unchanged. Those approaches focus on somewhat different aspects of the economy and reflect distinct ways of thinking about it. One approach addresses short-term effects that stem largely from variations in aggregate demand; the other addresses medium-term and long-term effects on the economy's potential output. Each approach represents people's economic decisions in a simplified way while capturing some important aspects of their behavior. (For additional details on the approaches, see Appendix A.)

The three paths do not incorporate any assumptions about the particular mix of spending or revenue changes used to accomplish increases or reductions in deficits and are not meant to correspond to any specific legislative proposals. Therefore, CBO assumed that each path would have the same marginal tax rates as those under current law. Because the unspecified policies that differentiate the paths were assumed to have no direct effect on the incentives to work and save, they differ in their economic effects only because of differences in the magnitude of budget deficits; those differences affect the economy primarily by altering the demand for goods and services in the next few years and national saving and investment later in the decade and beyond.

In estimating the short-run economic effects of those unspecified policies for deficit reduction, CBO assumed for its central estimates that each $1 change in primary budget deficits relative to those under current law would change output cumulatively by $1 over several quarters. That dollar-for-dollar response lies within the ranges of estimated effects on GDP of many policies examined in CBO's analysis of the macroeconomic effects of the American Recovery and Reinvestment Act of 2009 (ARRA). For its full range of estimates, CBO assumed that each $1 change in primary deficits would change output cumulatively by between $0.33 and $1.67. That range of possible effects on output, reflecting the uncertainty surrounding the possible outcomes, is about the same (in percentage terms) as the range between low and high estimates of the effects on output of particular policies in the analysis of ARRA.[5]

In this analysis, CBO reports effects of fiscal policy on GNP and the interest rate on 10-year Treasury notes. Changes in GNP are a better measure of the effects on U.S. residents' income than are changes in GDP—the more common measure of the economy's output. Because larger budget deficits generate larger inflows of capital from other countries, they imply that a growing portion of the nation's income would have to be sent abroad as returns (in the form of profits or interest) on that invested capital and thus would not be available to U.S. households. GNP would reflect such developments.

CBO did not estimate the effects of the paths on employment and unemployment. In general, if changes in budget deficits raise output in the short term, they will also raise employment and lower the unemployment rate. In the longer term, the economy is assumed to be operating near or at its maximum sustainable level, so changes in output caused by changes in budget deficits will be reflected primarily in productivity and wages rather than employment and unemployment (although changes in after-tax wages would have some effect on participation in the labor force and employment).

As in previous analyses of this sort, CBO has estimated the budgetary implications of the illustrative paths' macroeconomic effects using a simplified approach that takes into account the effects of changes in GNP, interest rates, and other factors.[6] Those effects include the following, for example: Higher output implies higher taxable incomes and, therefore, increased tax revenues; and higher interest rates imply greater interest payments on the public debt and, therefore, more spending.

Macroeconomic Effects of Changes in Budget Deficits

According to CBO's baseline economic projections, real GNP under current law will grow by 1.3 percent in 2013 (as measured by the change from the fourth quarter of the previous year) and by 3.3 percent in 2014. Economic growth is then projected to pick up further, and the economy is projected to reach its productive capacity in 2017 and continue to grow in line with the increase in that capacity thereafter. According to CBO's estimates, Path 1, which would increase deficits in comparison to the budgetary outcomes under current law, would increase output in the next few years and decrease it in later years compared with the economic outcomes under current law. Paths 2 and 3, which would reduce deficits, would reduce output in the next few years and increase it in later years compared with current-law economic outcomes.

Those estimated effects on output incorporate the impact of the paths on interest rates. Under Path 1, interest rates would rise, and those effects would become larger over

---

5. See Congressional Budget Office, *Estimated Impact of the American Recovery and Reinvestment Act on Employment and Economic Output from July 2012 Through September 2012* (November 2012).

6. For examples of such previous work, see Congressional Budget Office, *The Economic Impact of the President's 2013 Budget* (April 2012), and *The Macroeconomic and Budgetary Effects of an Illustrative Policy for Reducing the Federal Budget Deficit* (July 2011).

Figure 2.

Effects of Illustrative Paths on Real GNP, Calendar Years 2013 to 2023, Relative to Projections Under Current Law

(Percentage difference from baseline)

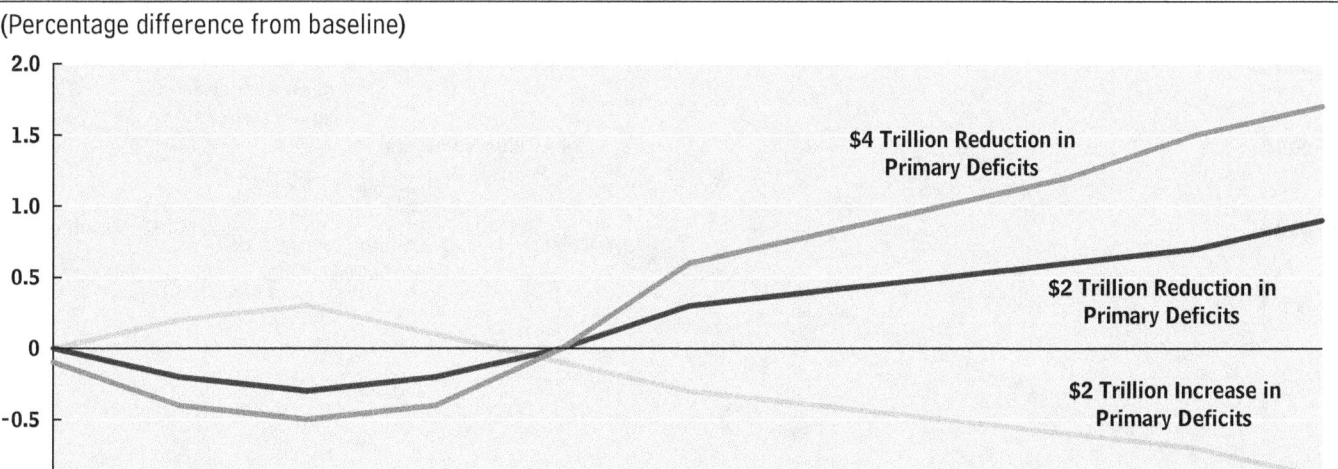

Source: Congressional Budget Office.

Notes: The illustrative paths are described in detail in the text, at the beginning of the section titled "Budget Deficits Under Three Illustrative Paths."

The primary deficit equals revenues minus noninterest spending.

Figures reflect the percentage difference in the annual levels between a path's effects and the outcomes under CBO's baseline, which incorporates the assumption that current laws generally remain unchanged.

Real GNP = inflation-adjusted gross national product.

time—primarily because deficits under Path 1 would be larger than those under current law, and the resulting reduction in national saving would raise the returns on capital investments. Under Paths 2 and 3, interest rates would be lower than those under current law, and those effects would become larger over time, reflecting increasing deficit reduction.

For all of the paths, the effects on output and interest rates at the end of the coming decade would generally continue to grow in later years. However, those longer-term effects would depend on the precise way that policies were extended after 2023.

Effects on Gross National Product from 2014 to 2023

CBO estimates that, relative to current law, policies that raised spending and cut taxes would lead to higher deficits and higher GNP from 2014 to 2016, and policies that cut spending and raised taxes would lead to lower deficits and lower GNP from 2014 to 2016, reflecting the short-term impact of tax and spending policies on the

demand for goods and services (see Figure 2). By contrast, CBO estimates that sustained higher deficits would lead to lower GNP beginning in 2017 and that sustained lower deficits would lead to higher GNP beginning in 2017, reflecting the impact of deficits on national saving and domestic investment (and without accounting for any changes to households' incentives to work or save stemming from the changes to tax policies or benefit programs).

Path 1: A $2 Trillion Increase in Primary Deficits.
Because CBO estimates that the unspecified policies increasing the deficit by $2 trillion relative to that under current law would increase aggregate demand in the near term, real GNP would be 0.3 percent higher in the fourth quarter of 2014 than the amount under current law (see Table 1 on page 4).

That figure represents CBO's central estimate, which is based on the assumption that the values for key aspects of economic behavior (in particular, the extent to which higher aggregate demand brought about by the

Figure 3.

Real GNP per Person Under CBO's Baseline and Illustrative Paths, Calendar Years 2014 to 2023

(2005 dollars)

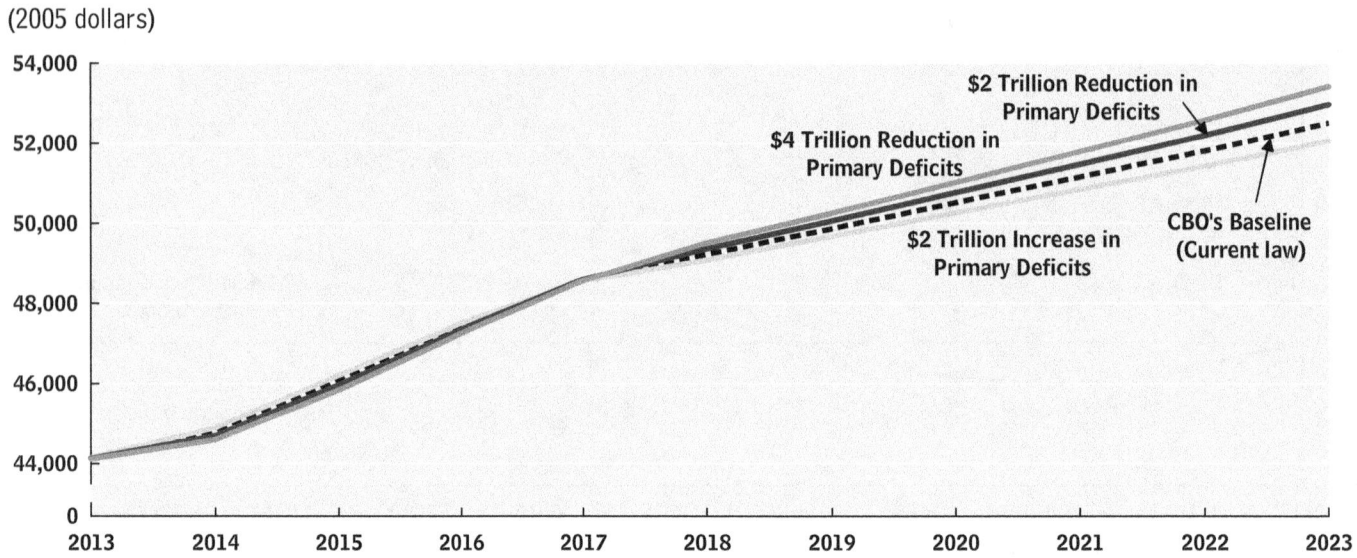

Source: Congressional Budget Office.

Notes: The illustrative paths are described in detail in the text, at the beginning of the section titled "Budget Deficits Under Three Illustrative Paths."

The primary deficit equals revenues minus noninterest spending.

Real GNP = inflation-adjusted gross national product.

unspecified policies would lead to further changes in the economy) are the midpoints of estimated ranges. The full ranges that CBO uses for those parameters suggest that real GNP would be between 0.1 percent and 0.5 percent higher in the fourth quarter of 2014 than the amount under current law. However, the macroeconomic impact of changes in fiscal policy could lie outside the ranges of estimates reported here for this path as well as the others, depending on the future state of the economy, the responses of households and businesses to the policies, and numerous other factors.

In 2023, real GNP would be 0.9 percent lower than that under current law (or between 0.5 percent and 1.3 percent lower, under CBO's full range of assumptions). Larger deficits would reduce national saving and "crowd out" domestic investment (as savings that would otherwise fund private investment were instead used to purchase government debt)—lowering output. However, even with the negative impact of fiscal policy under this path, real GNP per person would be considerably higher in 2023 than it is now because of continued growth in labor productivity (see Figure 3).

Path 2: A $2 Trillion Reduction in Primary Deficits. By CBO's estimates, the unspecified policies reducing the deficit by $2 trillion relative to that under current law would decrease aggregate demand in the near term. As a result, real GNP would be 0.3 percent lower in the fourth quarter of 2014 than the amount under current law, CBO projects (or between 0.1 percent and 0.5 percent lower under CBO's full range of assumptions).

In 2023, real GNP would be 0.9 percent higher than the outcome under current law (or between 0.5 percent and 1.3 percent higher under CBO's full range of assumptions), as the effects of Path 1 are reversed: Smaller deficits would increase national saving and boost domestic investment, raising output.

Path 3: A $4 Trillion Reduction in Primary Deficits. Under this path, the effects on output would be double those under Path 2 because of the greater reduction in deficits. Real GNP would be 0.6 percent lower in the fourth quarter of 2014 than the amount under current law (or between 0.2 percent and 1.0 percent lower under CBO's full range of assumptions).

Table 3.

Effects of Illustrative Paths on Interest Rates on 10-Year Treasury Notes in Selected Calendar Years, Relative to Projections Under Current Law

(Percentage-point difference)

	Short Term (2014)	Longer Term (2023)
$2 Trillion Increase in Primary Deficits		
Central estimate	*	0.1
Range	* to 0.1	0.1 to 0.2
$2 Trillion Reduction in Primary Deficits		
Central estimate	*	-0.1
Range	*	-0.2 to -0.1
$4 Trillion Reduction in Primary Deficits		
Central estimate	-0.1	-0.2
Range	-0.1 to *	-0.4 to -0.1

Source:　Congressional Budget Office.

Notes:　The illustrative paths are described in detail in the text, at the beginning of the section titled "Budget Deficits Under Three Illustrative Paths."

The primary deficit equals revenues minus noninterest spending.

Figures reflect the percentage-point difference (in the fourth quarter levels) between a path's effects and the outcomes under CBO's baseline, which incorporates the assumption that current laws generally remain unchanged.

Ranges of estimated effects are shown to reflect the uncertainty that exists about many of the economic relationships that are important in the models used to calculate those effects.

The effects on rates of an increase in the deficit are larger than those of an equal-sized decrease in the deficit. See Appendix A for details.

* = between -0.05 and 0.05.

In 2023, real GNP would be 1.7 percent higher than the amount under current law (or between 0.9 percent and 2.5 percent higher under CBO's full range of assumptions). Particularly relevant for this path, a reduction of $4 trillion in the cumulative primary deficit relative to what would occur under current law would be very difficult to accomplish without directly changing incentives to work and save.

Effects on 10-Year Treasury Interest Rates from 2014 to 2023

Path 1 would tend to increase interest rates relative to CBO's baseline projections through two main channels. First, the path implies a higher cumulative deficit over the next 10 years than the outcome under current law. That higher cumulative deficit would lead to higher long-term interest rates every year because investment would be crowded out. Second, compared with current law, Path 1 would induce greater economic activity in the near term,

which would lead the Federal Reserve to raise short-term interest rates somewhat sooner and to scale back other policies holding down long-term interest rates. As a result, the interest rate on 10-year Treasury securities would be a touch higher in 2014 than the rate under current law and 0.1 percentage point higher in 2023 (or as much as 0.2 percentage points higher under CBO's full range of assumptions) (see Table 3).

Paths 2 and 3 would have the opposite effects, resulting in lower interest rates than those under current law. Under Path 2, the interest rate on 10-year Treasury securities would be a bit lower than that under current law in 2014 and 0.1 percentage point lower in 2023 (or as much as 0.2 percentage points lower under CBO's full range of assumptions). Under Path 3, the interest rate on 10-year Treasury securities would be 0.1 percentage point lower than that under current law in 2014 and 0.2 percentage points lower in 2023 (or between 0.1 percentage point

Table 4.

Effects of Illustrative Paths on the Cumulative Deficit for Fiscal Years 2014 to 2023, With and Without Economic Effects, Relative to Projections Under Current Law

(Billions of dollars)

	Cumulative Deficit Without Economic Effects	Cumulative Budgetary Impact of Economic Effects	Cumulative Deficit With Economic Effects
	Increases (−) in Deficits		
$2 Trillion Increase in Primary Deficits			
Effect on primary deficits	-2,000	-71	-2,071
Debt service	-322	-79	-401
Effect on total deficits	-2,322	-151	-2,472
	Decreases (+) in Deficits		
$2 Trillion Reduction in Primary Deficits			
Effect on primary deficits	2,000	47	2,047
Debt service	322	57	378
Effect on total deficits	2,322	103	2,425
$4 Trillion Reduction in Primary Deficits			
Effect on primary deficits	4,000	92	4,092
Debt service	643	94	737
Effect on total deficits	4,643	186	4,829

Source: Congressional Budget Office.

Notes: The illustrative paths are described in detail in the text, at the beginning of the section titled "Budget Deficits Under Three Illustrative Paths."

The primary deficit equals revenues minus noninterest spending. Debt service is the change in the deficit that would result from changes in the amount of interest paid on the public debt (including the effects of changes in interest rates). The effect on total deficits is the sum of the effects on primary deficits and debt service.

Negative numbers indicate that deficits under the path are larger than those under CBO's baseline, which incorporates the assumption that current laws generally remain unchanged; positive amounts indicate that deficits are smaller.

The effects on output and interest rates of an increase in the deficit are larger than those of an equal-sized decrease in the deficit. As a result, the budgetary impact of the economic effects is greater for Path 1 than for Path 2. In addition, the effects of a bigger decrease in the deficit are proportionally smaller than the effects of a smaller decrease. See Appendix A for details.

and 0.4 percentage points lower under CBO's full range of assumptions).

The Budgetary Impact of the Macroeconomic Effects

The economic effects described above would "feed back" to the budget and affect the size of deficits. CBO has estimated those implications for the budget over fiscal years 2014 to 2023 using a simplified analysis that takes into account changes in taxable incomes and interest rates, among other things, but does not incorporate a detailed program-by-program analysis, as do CBO's regular bud-

get projections. Most of the estimated effects that the paths would have on the budget stem from two factors:

- Changes in output would affect revenues by altering the amount of taxable incomes and

- Changes in deficits and thus the amount of debt (because of that change in revenues) and changes in interest rates would affect the federal government's interest payments, often known as debt service.

However, CBO's estimates also account for other effects, such as the impact of changes in prices on federal spending on purchases and transfer payments; the impact of

Figure 4.

Effects of Illustrative Paths on the Cumulative Deficit for Fiscal Years 2014 to 2023, With and Without Economic Effects, Relative to Projections Under Current Law

(Billions of dollars)

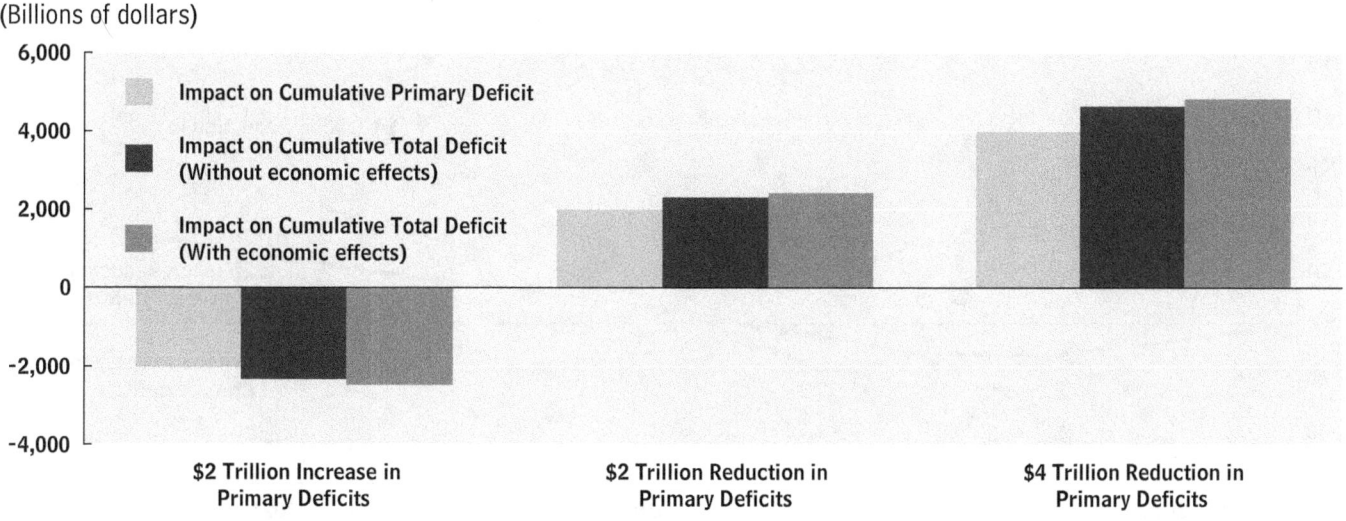

Source: Congressional Budget Office.

Notes: The illustrative paths are described in detail in the text, at the beginning of the section titled "Budget Deficits Under Three Illustrative Paths."

The primary deficit equals revenues minus noninterest spending. Debt service is the change in the deficit that would result from changes in the amount of interest paid on the public debt (including the effects of changes in interest rates). The effect on total deficits is the sum of the effects on primary deficits and debt service.

Negative numbers indicate that deficits under the path are larger than those under CBO's baseline, which incorporates the assumption that current laws generally remain unchanged; positive amounts indicate that deficits are smaller.

the unemployment rate on federal spending on unemployment benefits; and the impact of the mix of taxable incomes on revenues.

Cumulative Effects

For each path, CBO constructed the impact on primary deficits without including economic effects on the budget; calculated the impact on debt service and thus total deficits (again without economic feedback); estimated the macroeconomic effects of those changes in total deficits; estimated the budgetary impact of those macroeconomic effects (including effects on both primary deficits and debt service); and summed up the total impact on the budget, including debt service and economic effects, over fiscal years 2014 to 2023. The results are the following:

■ *Path 1: A $2 Trillion Increase in Primary Deficits.* Additional debt service would add a cumulative $0.3 trillion to the budgetary cost over that period

(before accounting for the economic effects), and economic effects would add $0.2 trillion (see Table 4). Altogether, the cumulative total deficit would be $2.5 trillion higher over fiscal years 2014 to 2023, CBO estimates (see Figure 4). As a result, debt held by the public would rise to 87 percent of GDP in 2023, compared with 73 percent at the end of fiscal year 2012 and 77 percent projected for 2023 under current law.

Path 2: A $2 Trillion Reduction in Primary Deficits. Lower interest costs would subtract an additional $0.3 trillion from the deficit (before accounting for the economic effects), and economic effects would subtract another $0.1 trillion. Altogether, the cumulative total deficit would be $2.4 trillion lower over fiscal years 2014 to 2023, CBO estimates. Debt held by the public would decline to 67 percent of GDP in 2023.

Figure 5.

Budgetary Impact of Economic Effects of Illustrative Paths, Fiscal Years 2013 to 2023, Relative to Projections Under Current Law

(Billions of dollars)

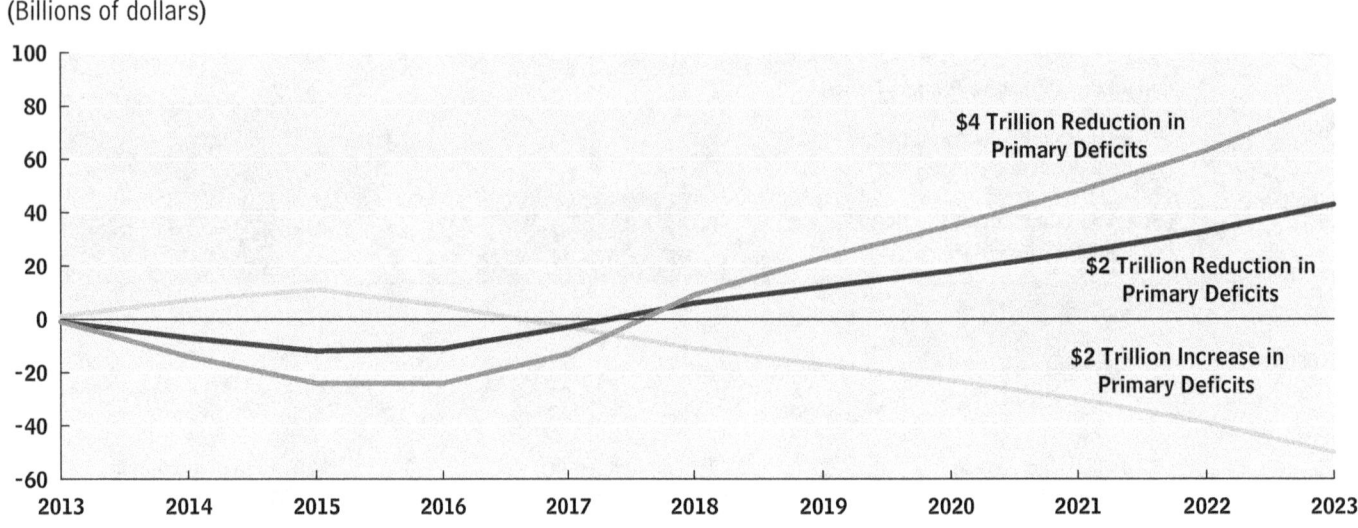

Source: Congressional Budget Office.

Notes: The illustrative paths are described in detail in the text, at the beginning of the section titled "Budget Deficits Under Three Illustrative Paths."

The primary deficit equals revenues minus noninterest spending. Debt service is the change in the deficit that would result from changes in the amount of interest paid on the public debt (including the effects of changes in interest rates). The budgetary impact of economic effects is the sum of the effects on primary deficits and debt service.

Negative numbers indicate that deficits under the path are larger than those under CBO's baseline, which incorporates the assumption that current laws generally remain unchanged; positive amounts indicate that deficits are smaller.

■ *Path 3: A $4 Trillion Reduction in Primary Deficits.* Lower interest costs would subtract an additional $0.6 trillion from the deficit (before accounting for the economic effects), and economic effects would subtract $0.2 trillion. All told, the cumulative total deficit would be $4.8 trillion lower over fiscal years 2014 to 2023, CBO estimates. Debt held by the public would decline to 58 percent of GDP in 2023.

Differences in Impact Over Time

The impact of economic effects on the budget would vary over time because of the different magnitude of the changes in the deficit and the projected improvement in the economy over time (under current law and any of the paths). In the short term under Path 1, output would be higher than that under current law, short-term interest rates would remain close to zero, and long-term interest rates would be little changed. Together, those short-term economic effects of Path 1 would reduce budget deficits in the next few years. For example, under Path 1, although the policy change without economic effects

would boost the deficit by $40 billion in 2014, the economic effects of that change would offset about $7 billion of that increase. (See Figure 5; for additional detail on those effects and for estimates of the annual budgetary changes under each path, with and without economic effects, see Appendix B.)

Paths 2 and 3 would have similar short-term effects in the opposite direction. They would reduce output in the short run, and their economic effects would therefore tend to increase budget deficits in the next few years. For example, the economic effects of the budget policies under Path 2 would increase the deficit by $7 billion in fiscal year 2014, offsetting a portion of the $40 billion reduction assumed in the primary deficit; the economic effects of the budget policies under Path 3 would increase the total deficit by $14 billion in fiscal year 2014.

In the longer term, budgetary feedback effects would be driven primarily by changes in the cumulative deficit. A larger cumulative deficit such as that under Path 1 would tend to reduce output, with corresponding effects on taxable incomes. In addition, a larger deficit would tend to reduce national saving and thereby reduce the ratio of capital to labor, which would increase interest rates and thereby raise interest costs. Those factors would tend to worsen budget outcomes in later years under Path 1. Paths 2 and 3, which would reduce the cumulative deficit, would produce economic effects that improved budget outcomes over the longer term.

Economic and budgetary effects of fiscal policy are partly determined by the speed with which fiscal policy affects taxes and spending over time. For Paths 2 and 3, CBO chose budgetary paths that would reduce deficits by grad-

ually rising amounts relative to those under current law, beginning in 2014. Of course, different timing for changes in budget policies is possible. The longer that significant deficit reduction is deferred, the larger the government's accumulated debt will be (with its associated costs and risks), and the greater the policy changes will need to be when deficit reduction begins. Conversely, the sooner that the deficit is cut, the more the economic effects will be felt when the economy is still relatively weak, and the less time that households, businesses, and state and local governments will have to plan and adjust their behavior. In addition, the timing of the steps taken to put fiscal policy on a sustainable course will affect different generations differently.

Appendix A:
How CBO Estimated the Economic and Budgetary Effects of the Illustrative Paths

The Congressional Budget Office (CBO) used two approaches to estimate the effects of the illustrative paths on the economy relative to the agency's baseline projections. Those approaches focus on somewhat different aspects of the economy and reflect distinct ways of thinking about it. One approach addresses short-term effects that stem largely from variations in aggregate demand; the other addresses medium-term and long-term effects on the economy's potential output. Each approach represents people's economic decisions in a simplified way while capturing some important aspects of actual behavior.

In CBO's judgment, the macroeconomic effects of the paths would be determined primarily by effects on the demand for goods and services in 2014, by effects on the nation's capital stock (including such things as factories and computers) and the labor supply in 2018 and beyond, and by a combination of those factors from 2015 through 2017.[1] CBO has estimated the economic effects of the paths relative to the agency's February 2013 baseline economic forecast, which incorporates the assumption that current laws generally remain in place.[2]

Short-Term Economic Effects

CBO analyzes the short-term economic effects of changes in fiscal policy by using models and historical evidence to estimate the direct and indirect effects of budget policies on the economy. Direct effects change output by influencing the demand for goods and services, by either the federal government or the people and organizations directly affected by a policy—for example, the recipients of a tax cut. The size of a direct effect depends on a tax or spending provision's impact on the behavior of recipients. For example, if someone receives a tax reduction of a dollar and spends 80 cents (saving the other 20 cents), and production increases over time to meet the additional demand generated by that spending, the direct impact on output is 80 cents. The size of the direct effect, per dollar of budgetary cost, varies depending on the persistence of a policy (for example, whether it is permanent or temporary) and the characteristics of those affected by the policy (for example, whether the recipient of a tax cut or transfer has high or low income); in general, direct effects per dollar of budgetary cost are between zero and 1.0.[3]

Indirect effects enhance or offset direct effects. For example, the direct effects of lower taxes or higher spending are magnified when stronger demand for goods and services prompts companies to increase investment. In the other direction, direct effects are muted if higher government borrowing caused by tax decreases or spending increases leads to higher interest rates that discourage spending by households and businesses. With a large amount of

---

1. Specifically, CBO combines results from its modeling approaches as follows: estimates for 2013 and 2014 are based entirely on effects on demand; estimates for 2015, 2016, and 2017 place weights of 0.75, 0.50, and 0.25, respectively, on the effects on demand and the remaining weights on the effects on the capital stock and labor supply; and estimates for 2018 and beyond are based entirely on effects on the capital stock and labor supply.

2. See Congressional Budget Office, *The Budget and Economic Outlook: Fiscal Years 2013 to 2023* (February 2013).

3. For a review of the ranges of short-term economic impact that CBO estimates for different types of specific policies, see Congressional Budget Office, *Economic Effects of Policies Contributing to Fiscal Tightening in 2013* (November 2012).

unused resources in the U.S. economy today and over the next few years, CBO estimates that the indirect effects probably enhance the direct effects, on balance. Those additional effects can be represented by a demand multiplier, defined as the total change in output per dollar of direct effect on demand. Because there is considerable uncertainty about the economic relationships underlying indirect effects, CBO used estimates of that demand multiplier under current economic conditions ranging from 0.5 to 2.5, with a central estimate of 1.5, encompassing a broad range of economists' views.[4]

In addition, CBO made particular assumptions for the effects of the unspecified budgetary changes in the illustrative paths. CBO's analysis allowed those changes to have a range of effects on output. The medium-sized response reflects the assumption that each budgetary change of $1 would result in a direct effect of 67 cents and, including indirect effects, would change output cumulatively by $1 over several quarters.[5] At one end of the range, each $1 increase in the deficit was assumed to cause economic output to rise by a cumulative $0.33. At the opposite end of the range, each $1 increase in the deficit was assumed to cause economic output to rise by a cumulative $1.67.

The monetary policy of the Federal Reserve has an important influence on the economic effects of changes in taxes and government spending. CBO's estimates in this analysis incorporate the assumption that over the next several years, with short-term interest rates near zero, unemployment elevated, and inflation low, the Federal Reserve's response to changes in fiscal policy will be limited. That assumption implies that the short-run impact of fiscal policy on the economy is larger than would be the case under more usual economic conditions, when, for example, the Federal Reserve would probably increase short-term interest rates in response to cuts in taxes or increases in government spending.

---

4. For a discussion of CBO's approach to analyzing the short-term effects of fiscal policy, see Felix Reichling and Charles Whalen, *Assessing the Short-Term Effects on Output of Changes in Federal Fiscal Policies*, Congressional Budget Office Working Paper 2012-08 (May 2012).

5. For the purpose of this analysis, CBO assumed that 75 percent of the overall direct effect from unspecified budgetary changes would occur in the quarter when the change in the deficit occurred and 25 percent would occur in the following quarter.

A higher cumulative deficit over the long term under Path 1 would tend to boost long-term interest rates relative to those under current law as a higher cumulative deficit crowded out national saving available for investment. That effect would reduce the ratio of capital to labor in the economy in the long run, which would tend to increase the return on capital investments and, therefore, interest rates. Those long-run implications imply changes in interest rates even in the short run; long-term interest rates reflect, to at least some extent, the expectations that participants in financial markets have about future short-term rates. As a result, the expectation of an increase in interest rates as much as a decade in the future raises the interest rate on 10-year Treasury securities today. Policies that increased deficits over the next decade would engender such a reaction. In addition, the Federal Reserve would respond in a way that would increase long-term interest rates a little relative to the rates in CBO's baseline projections in the near term and thereby slightly attenuate the positive near-term economic effects of those policies. Because Paths 2 and 3 would reduce deficits, they would have the opposite effects on long-run interest rates in both the short run and the long run.

Fiscal policies might also affect spending by individuals and businesses by altering people's uncertainty or confidence about future economic conditions or government policies. Many firms appear to be uncertain today about future demand for their products, and that uncertainty seems to be leading them to be cautious about increasing their investment and hiring. Fiscal policy actions that would boost demand might lessen that uncertainty and increase employment.[6] However, such actions might also increase uncertainty about longer-run fiscal policy, which could have an opposing effect. Because quantifying such reactions to changes in fiscal policy would be extremely difficult, this report does not incorporate them.

Although the details of the changes to deficits under the illustrative paths in this report are not specified, the paths reflect the assumption that the underlying fiscal policies are credible, putting aside the effects of any potential doubts regarding the policies. Nevertheless, it is worth noting that households, businesses, state and local governments, and participants in the financial markets would be more likely to believe that intended deficit

---

6. See Nicholas Bloom, "The Impact of Uncertainty Shocks," *Econometrica*, vol. 77, no. 3 (May 2009), pp. 623–685.

reduction would truly take effect in the future if specific and widely supported policy changes were enacted into law in advance.

Medium-Term and Long-Term Economic Effects

In estimating the effects of deficits beyond the next few years, CBO uses an enhanced version of a widely used model developed by Robert Solow. In that model, output depends on the quantity and quality of the labor force, the size and composition of the capital stock, and the nation's technological progress.[7]

This analysis focused on how the illustrative paths would affect output and income by changing the nation's capital stock (through the magnitude of deficits) and the labor supply (through the pretax wage rate). For example, a path leading to projected debt higher than that implied by current law would tend to generate lower output and higher interest rates because of crowding out of capital investment. That reduction in capital investment would, in turn, lower pretax wage rates.

The capital stock owned by residents of the United States depends on national saving, which is the sum of personal saving, business saving (that is, after-tax corporate profits not paid as dividends), and saving or dissaving (as reflected in budget surpluses or deficits) by the federal government and state and local governments. Federal budget deficits reduce national saving, resulting in a smaller capital stock owned by U.S. residents over time from a decrease in domestic investment, an increase in net borrowing from abroad, or both. To reflect the high degree of uncertainty that attends those effects, CBO produced estimates of the economic effects of the illustrative paths using a range of assumptions about how each dollar increase in deficits would reduce domestic investment (reflecting different assumptions about the effects of deficits on both national saving and net borrowing from abroad):

■ A "large" investment response, under which each dollar increase in deficits would reduce domestic investment by 50 cents;

7. For details of that model and a discussion of alternative assumptions about the effects of budget deficits on saving and investment, see Congressional Budget Office, *The Economic Impact of the President's 2013 Budget* (April 2012), Appendix A.

■ A "small" investment response, under which each dollar increase in deficits would reduce domestic investment by 15 cents; and

■ A "medium" investment response, under which each dollar increase in deficits would reduce domestic investment by 33 cents.

The smaller capital stock that results from less investment would decrease economic output (because the labor force would have less capital and would therefore be less productive) and increase interest rates (because the greater scarcity of capital would drive up the cost of using it).

Productive investments by the government can also increase output by raising productivity in the private sector. However, the unspecified changes in deficits that differentiate the three paths were assumed to leave government investment unchanged.

To reflect the high degree of uncertainty that attends the effect of the wage rate on the supply of labor, CBO produced estimates of the economic effects of the illustrative budgetary paths using a range of assumptions about how people would adjust the number of hours they worked in response to changes in the wage rate:

■ A "strong" labor supply response, under which workers' response is on the high side of the range of empirical estimates;

■ A "weak" labor supply response, under which workers' response is on the low side of the range; and

■ A "medium" labor supply response, under which workers' response is roughly midway between strong and weak.

The responsiveness of the labor supply to wages is often expressed as the total wage elasticity (the change in total labor income caused by a 1 percent change in after-tax wages). The total wage elasticity, in turn, has two components: a substitution elasticity, which measures the effect of changes in the amount of additional income from each additional hour of work (applicable to an additional dollar of income) and an income elasticity, which measures the effect of changes in total income (the total tax liability divided by income). In this analysis, CBO's assumptions for the labor supply response correspond to total wage elasticities of about 0.32 for the strong response (composed of a substitution elasticity of 0.32 and an income elasticity of zero); about 0.06 for the weak response (composed of a substitution elasticity of 0.16 and an income elasticity of -0.10); and about 0.19 for the medium response (composed of a substitution elasticity of 0.24 and an income elasticity of -0.05).[8]

Asymmetries in Economic and Budgetary Effects

In the long run, an increase in deficits affects output more than does an equal-sized decrease, CBO estimates. Each additional increment to the capital stock raises GDP by a smaller amount. Consequently, even though positive and negative changes to the deficit are estimated to have symmetrical direct effects on capital investment, the resulting effects on output are not symmetrical: An increase in deficits (which shrinks the capital stock) has a proportionally greater effect on output than does an equal-sized reduction in deficits. (For the same reason, Path 3, under which the initial reduction in primary deficits is twice as large as that of Path 2, has effects on output that are less than twice as large.)

Similarly, an increase in deficits has a greater effect on interest rates than does an equal-sized decrease, for two reasons. First, with short-term interest rates currently near zero, they are more readily boosted by an increase in deficits than they are dampened by a decrease in deficits. Moreover, the bigger differences in the path of short-term rates after an increase in deficits imply bigger changes in long-term rates, even before those short-term rates begin to change. Second, the interest rate is more responsive to changes in the capital stock as the capital stock gets smaller. As a result, an increase in deficits has a proportionally larger effect on interest rates. (For the same reason, under Path 3, the effects on interest rates are less than twice as large as those under Path 2.)

The asymmetry in economic effects implies an asymmetry in budgetary effects. Higher deficits reduce output, and therefore taxable incomes, to a greater degree than lower deficits increase them; and higher deficits increase interest rates, and therefore interest payments, by more than lower deficits decrease them. Therefore, the eco-

nomic effects of higher deficits boost the deficit by a greater increment than the economic effects of lower deficits shrink the deficit. Over time, those budgetary effects, in turn, further affect the capital stock, magnifying the initial difference in the effects on output and interest rates.

Differences from Previous Estimates of Economic Effects

The estimated economic effects of a $2 trillion reduction in primary deficits presented in this report differ slightly from those CBO presented in July 2011 for several reasons.[9] First, on the basis of a continuing review of the evidence, CBO reduced its estimate of the "medium" investment response from 36 cents per dollar of deficit to 33 cents per dollar of deficit and reduced its "small" investment response from 20 cents per dollar of deficit to 15 cents per dollar of deficit. As a result of those revisions, both the central and most favorable estimates of the impact of reduced deficits on gross national product (GNP) are smaller than previously estimated.

In addition, for the current analysis, CBO assumed that deficit reduction would be phased in more slowly than was assumed in the 2011 report. That difference implies a smaller cumulative reduction in interest payments, also leading to a smaller estimated effect of deficit reduction on GNP.

Budgetary Impact of the Macroeconomic Effects

CBO estimated the budgetary implications of the macroeconomic effects of the illustrative paths using a simplified analysis that takes into account changes in taxable incomes and interest rates, among other things, but does not incorporate a detailed program-by-program analysis, as occurs for CBO's regular budget projections. Most of the estimated impact of the economic effects on the budget stems from changes in taxable incomes and interest rates.

Changes in output affect the budget through their impact on taxable incomes: Higher output implies higher taxable incomes—increasing revenues and reducing the deficit.

---

8. For details on CBO's assumptions about the impact of the wage rate on the labor supply, see Congressional Budget Office, *How the Supply of Labor Responds to Changes in Fiscal Policy* (October 2012).

9. Congressional Budget Office, *The Macroeconomic and Budgetary Effects of an Illustrative Policy for Reducing the Federal Budget Deficit* (July 2011).

In addition, economic growth can push taxpayers into higher tax brackets, so revenues tend to rise more than proportionally with taxable incomes. CBO's budget calculations for this analysis reflect features of U.S. tax laws that result in little U.S. tax effectively being imposed on foreign income of U.S. residents and much of the income earned in this country by foreign residents effectively being taxed here.

Interest rates affect the budget mostly through their impact on the government's interest payments on the national debt. But changes in interest rates are reflected in total interest costs only gradually, as new securities are issued at those higher rates. New securities must be sold to pay for the redemption of maturing securities and to finance additional borrowing because of larger deficits. Currently, about 23 percent of marketable federal debt held by the public has a maturity of two years or less.

Appendix B:
Further Details on Economic and Budgetary Effects

In this appendix, the Congressional Budget Office's (CBO's) estimate of the effects of each illustrative path on the primary deficit, net interest, and total deficits are shown relative to the projected outcomes under current law with economic effects included (see Table B-1). The differences between the estimates with and without economic effects included constitute the budgetary impact of the economic effects (see Table B-2).

The estimated effects of each path on gross domestic product (GDP) are shown for 2014 and 2023 relative to the projected outcomes under current law (see Table B-3). In general, the short-term effects are very similar to those on gross national product (GNP). In the longer run, the effects on GDP tend to be smaller than those on GNP. For example, according to CBO's central estimates, Path 3 would boost real (inflation-adjusted) GDP by 1.0 percent in 2023; in comparison, Path 3 would boost real GNP by 1.7 percent in 2023.

The differences between the effects on GDP and GNP reflect the consequences of changes in profits and interest payments sent abroad. Consider the effects of smaller budget deficits. First, those smaller deficits would generate smaller inflows of capital from other countries; as a result, a smaller portion of the nation's income would have to be sent abroad as returns (in the form of profits or interest) on that invested capital and thus would not be available to U.S. households. Second, those smaller deficits would lower interest rates, implying lower payments for each dollar of foreign-owned U.S. assets. Both of those effects would have a positive impact on GNP that would not be included in GDP. Similarly, for larger budget deficits, the negative impact on GNP would be larger than the negative impact on GDP.

Table B-1.

Effects of Illustrative Paths on the Budget With Economic Effects, Fiscal Years 2014 to 2023, Relative to Projections Under Current Law

(Billions of dollars)

	2014	2015	2016	2017	2018	2019	2020	2021	2022	2023	2014-2023
					Increases (-) in Deficits						
$2 Trillion Increase in Primary Deficits											
Effect on primary deficits	-33	-64	-103	-145	-188	-229	-268	-307	-347	-388	-2,071
Debt service	-1	-2	-7	-14	-25	-35	-49	-67	-88	-113	-401
Effect on Total Deficits	-34	-65	-110	-159	-213	-264	-317	-375	-436	-501	-2,472
					Decreases (+) in Deficits						
$2 Trillion Reduction in Primary Deficits											
Effect on primary deficits	33	63	99	141	185	226	265	304	345	386	2,047
Debt service	1	1	5	12	23	33	47	64	85	108	378
Effect on Total Deficits	33	65	104	153	208	259	312	369	429	494	2,425
$4 Trillion Reduction in Primary Deficits											
Effect on primary deficits	65	126	197	278	370	453	531	610	690	772	4,092
Debt service	2	3	9	21	42	64	92	127	166	212	737
Effect on Total Deficits	67	129	206	299	412	517	623	736	856	984	4,829
Memorandum:											
CBO's February 2013 Baseline											
Primary deficit (-) or surplus	-373	-158	-153	-123	-88	-117	-131	-123	-163	-120	-1,549
Net interest (-)	-243	-272	-323	-412	-517	-593	-667	-730	-795	-857	-5,410
Total Deficit	-616	-430	-476	-535	-605	-710	-798	-854	-957	-978	-6,958

Source: Congressional Budget Office.

Notes: The illustrative paths are described in detail in the text, at the beginning of the section titled "Budget Deficits Under Three Illustrative Paths."

The primary deficit equals revenues minus noninterest spending. Debt service is the change in the deficit that would result from changes in the amount of interest paid on the public debt (including the effects of changes in interest rates). The effect on total deficits is the sum of the effect on primary deficits and debt service.

Negative numbers indicate that deficits under the path are larger than those under CBO's baseline, which incorporates the assumption that current laws generally remain unchanged; positive amounts indicate that deficits are smaller.

The effects on output and interest rates of an increase in the deficit are larger than those of an equal-sized decrease in the deficit. As a result, the budgetary impact of the economic effects is greater for Path 1 and for Path 2. See Appendix A for details.

Table B-2.

Budgetary Impact of Economic Effects of Illustrative Paths, Fiscal Years 2014 to 2023, Relative to Projections Under Current Law

(Billions of dollars)

	2014	2015	2016	2017	2018	2019	2020	2021	2022	2023	2014-2023
				Increases (-) / Decreases (+) in Deficits							
$2 Trillion Increase in Primary Deficits											
Effect on primary deficits	7	12	8	2	-6	-11	-14	-18	-23	-28	-71
Debt service	-1	-1	-3	-5	-5	-6	-9	-12	-16	-22	-79
Effect on Total Deficits	7	11	5	-3	-11	-17	-23	-30	-39	-50	-151
$2 Trillion Reduction in Primary Deficits											
Effect on primary deficits	-7	-12	-12	-5	3	8	12	16	20	26	47
Debt service	1	1	1	2	3	4	6	9	13	17	57
Effect on Total Deficits	-7	-12	-11	-3	6	12	18	25	33	43	103
$4 Trillion Reduction in Primary Deficits											
Effect on primary deficits	-15	-25	-26	-15	6	17	24	32	41	52	92
Debt service	1	2	2	2	3	6	10	16	22	30	94
Effect on Total Deficits	-14	-24	-24	-13	9	23	35	48	63	82	186

Source: Congressional Budget Office.

Notes: The illustrative paths are described in detail in the text, at the beginning of the section titled "Budget Deficits Under Three Illustrative Paths."

The primary deficit equals revenues minus noninterest spending. Debt service is the change in the deficit that would result from changes in the amount of interest paid on the public debt (including the effects of changes in interest rates). The effect on total deficits is the sum of the effects on primary deficits and debt service.

Negative numbers indicate that deficits under the path are larger than those under CBO's baseline, which incorporates the assumption that current laws generally remain unchanged; positive amounts indicate that deficits are smaller.

The effects on output and interest rates of an increase in the deficit are larger than those of an equal-sized decrease in the deficit. As a result, the budgetary impact of the economic effects is greater for Path 1 and for Path 2. See Appendix A for details.

Table B-3.

Effects of Illustrative Paths on Real GDP in Selected Calendar Years, Relative to Projections Under Current Law

(Percentage difference)

	Short Term (2014)	Longer Term (2023)
$2 Trillion Increase in Primary Deficits		
Central estimate	0.3	-0.5
Range	0.1 to 0.5	-0.9 to -0.2
$2 Trillion Reduction in Primary Deficits		
Central estimate	-0.3	0.5
Range	-0.5 to -0.1	0.2 to 0.8
$4 Trillion Reduction in Primary Deficits		
Central estimate	-0.6	1.0
Range	-1.1 to -0.2	0.4 to 1.7

Source: Congressional Budget Office.

Notes: The illustrative paths are described in detail in the text, at the beginning of the section titled "Budget Deficits Under Three Illustrative Paths."

The primary deficit equals revenues minus noninterest spending.

Figures reflect the percentage difference in the fourth quarter levels between a path's effects and the outcomes under CBO's baseline, which incorporates the assumption that current laws generally remain unchanged.

Ranges of estimated effects are shown to reflect the uncertainty that exists about many of the economic relationships that are important in the models used to calculate those effects.

The effects on GDP of an increase in the deficit are larger than those of a decrease in the deficit. See Appendix A for details.

Real GDP = inflation-adjusted gross domestic product.

List of Tables and Figures

About This Document

This Congressional Budget Office (CBO) report was prepared at the request of the Chairman of the Senate Budget Committee. In keeping with CBO's mandate to provide objective, impartial analysis, the report makes no recommendations.

Benjamin Page wrote the report, under the direction of Wendy Edelberg. The underlying economic and budgetary analysis was conducted by Jared Brewster, Jonathan Huntley, Felix Reichling, Frank Russek, and Bob Shackleton. Robert Greenstein of the Center on Budget and Policy Priorities and Douglas Holtz-Eakin of the American Action Forum provided helpful comments. The assistance of external reviewers implies no responsibility for the final product, which rests solely with CBO.

John Skeen edited the report, and Maureen Costantino and Jeanine Rees prepared it for publication. An electronic version is available on CBO's Web site www.cbo.gov.

Douglas W. Elmendorf
Director

February 2013